VIRGA

VIRGA

JENNIFER HOULE

Garry Thomas Morse, Editor

Cover design by Doowah Design.
Photo of Jennifer Houle by Mag Hood.

This book was printed on Ancient Forest Friendly paper.
Printed and bound in Canada by Marquis Book Printing.

We acknowledge the support of The Canada Council for the Arts and the Manitoba Arts Council for our publishing program.

Library and Archives Canada Cataloguing in Publication

Title: Virga / Jennifer Houle.
Names: Houle, Jennifer, 1977- author.
Description: Poems.
Identifiers: Canadiana 20190057742 | ISBN 9781773240466 (softcover)
Classification: LCC PS8615.O8498 V57 2019 | DDC C811/.6—dc23

Signature Editions
P.O. Box 206, RPO Corydon, Winnipeg, Manitoba, R3M 3S7
www.signature-editions.com

For Kim, Liz, Meg, and Nat

Virga:
Rain that evaporates before it touches ground;
a cloud formation often seen on the horizon.

The word "virga" is etymologically related
to the Latin for "stick" or "rod."

Passed years seem safe ones, vanquished ones, while the future lives in a cloud, formidable from a distance. The cloud clears as you enter it.

— Beryl Markham

Waterfall

You watch me emerge from behind
the plume. No need to speak

of vulnerabilities. Water nymph, dryad,
ancient high goddess. Muse of our brook.

Enchantress, we settle on. Lady of.

You have said nothing about new wrinkles.
Given deep scars, you whisper: and?

On top, soft as ever, dew on your skin,
all over your hands.

How did you ever come to give me
such strong dreams, to look toward

the entrance to the self, so often lost,
until my own gaze follows

that ragged cave
that twig-littered drop

there it is now
through sun-shocked

mist. Remember.

The Lost Pleiad

My indignant sisters said: don't go,
you idiot. You don't need us to tell you

what will happen. We need you here to help
with things, besides – our work, the fountains,

father in his weariness, mother losing time.
You were always selfish, scribbling

impertinent questions to sky gods
while nebulae boiled over, leaving

gouache and scales to us. First,
you should learn to keep your room.

Keep even one star lit.

o

But I had seen a woman meet a man
in a dim, stone corridor, light bulb

swaying, hair mussed, loose tee
off the shoulder, glittering straps

and collarbone, oculi and angles,
fingers, tongues. Resurgent

hunger. Silence that knew well
it was a waste of breath to ask.

A world of cold streets, colder
offices, icicles suspended

from exhaust pipes, windshields
layered with hard snow. A man

who'd chip away to make it places
he did not care if he got, hunched

over sketched mountaintops
he did not know he drew.

He'd go for walks alone and talk
to no one, keep out of the crowds

and leave clubs early, bored,
in no kind of a mood for his own lies.

o

Down

a wet
rope-

ladder. Gut
braided with hemp

and fishing line,
scarves

clotted with clay,
oil, blood,

the long, wet
hair of heroines

gone missing,
drowned,

snagged in sisal,
jute,

swan feather
and quail plume.

Stubbed toes sliding
into pulp and lovers'

knots, down
the gnarled serpents,

slick with moss,
into muscled body,

into storms of words
and names, a mess

of codes,
coordinates,

lists, maps,
and personal

numbers.

Derivative

I am of Gaul. Of Sicily and chestnut trees, of outside Montreal.
I am of the left-field, a curveball, changing all who held me

bawling, blessed. Fell from the stars. Maybe. My six sisters weep
in autumn from the shoulder of the bull, trailed by Aldebaran,

urging me home to reignite a darkened star with gaslight. God.
I am of Acadie, a sinking island, Massachusetts, old green deities,

candles to call love back from beyond. I am of the haunted
willows, pewter rings and pentagrams – mourner of the drowned,

keeper of arnica root in what is Danvers now. I am of County Donegal.
I am of the sand upon this sickly shore. I am of the factory slum,

of festivals and feast days, cigarettes and scholarships, ways out.
I am of the forest people, of the shining birches, narrow paths

in autumn, of the patted, patched folkloric, of the fairies, oak and ash,
cluster of hamadryads, of lured, drawn Arianrhod – dashed, of ninefold

Blodeuwedd. Of bee stung lip, of flower face, of sparkling rivulet
reflecting hanging blooms of cone, of ample breasts and beds of needle leaf,

the pricked young skin of craving. *Let me go.* I am of the hardest, longest
burning woods, of cold nights waiting out the danger, young September,

dark-haired, swarthy ally of the mist, of fog, of cottage stove, of wild rose.
I am of working mothers, diplomats and doctors, firsts to be admitted,

to divorce, want something better, lose a language, take another tongue,
to dash their blinding names upon wet rocks. To graduate. Heretics. Advertisers.

I am any. I am either. Tallest woman in a family of short women. I'm 5'5.
Soberest, most wary, prone to visions of my own. I am of the Celtic knot,

mortar and pestle, seawater and sulphur. Daughter of a street kid, I came hard,
a heathen after centuries of Catholics. Firstborn girl of warring strangers,

I crowned into trouble. I was trouble. Here she comes, the rotten kid.
I am of the beautiful, the lost. I am of paint and hardware stores, of gardens

and small airports, of young summertimes away. Once I was rich, and I flew open
into storm, and I was caught. There were no universities. The world held

only mirrors, shopping malls, and sex. So I was lost. Turned. And lost again.
Returned, navigating ice and hormone surge, I came through gasping uterus,

cracked pelvis, shattered collarbone and ribs. Returned through pill and liniment, through
traffic, and unrest, and crushing debt. I came and went, went nowhere fast. But read.

I have come to venture one more guess. I am December born, of star and goat and fish,
of whirled and flung triskelion, of willful, lucky devils – of improbable ascents.

Filmography

Waitress, maid,

mourner, woman, waitress,
woman, voter, clerk, waitress,
victim, waitress, mourner,
woman, mother, waitress, shopper,
stand-in, double, mother, stripper,
sister, mother, hooker, Jenny,

mother, maid, mother, nurse
assistant, waitress, mother,
debtor, mother, nurse, helper,
daughter, client, waitress, teller,
mother, patient, mourner,
mother, waitress, shopper,
clerk, mourner, girl, suspect,

singer, parent, angry mother, other
dancer, taxi hailer, girl in crowd,
Andrew's girlfriend, bitch in bar,
waitress, girl, girl, girl, girl, girl,

poor candidate, cashier.

Fomalhaut[1]

The mouth of the fish
pierced by a hook

bleeds reddish light
from 1989

how lonely you were then
to bite

cut off from a family
that could not hold you back

The order that you made
from such debris,

bright belts of your disks
still wanting to wander

as you ushered them around
your hidden answers.

You never were the light
of our best days,

keeping your own counsel,
a facet of lengthening night.

I was solitary too,
a bullied twelve when first

I saw what you endured
and let you blur, alone

within your wordless fire.
Now I look again.

1 *With ancient associations to the winter solstice, remote Fomalhaut is the brightest star in the Austrina Piscis constellation, also known as the Southern Fish, or the Lonely One. It has its own planetary system, where astronomers discovered the first visible exoplanet in 2008. Maybe not so lonely after all.*

Part 1: Final Girl

Every night I hurtle from another forest,
naked under weathered work shirt,

barefoot after violent misadventure.
Touch my children and you'll see. Touch me.

Oh, don't laugh. I've already killed,
disrupted coitus, plotted for love and lives

to unravel, lives that kept me in the depths,
kicking in the lake of their missteps –

growing resourceful, sucking my
skinny wrist for its salt.

Part 2: The Pretty One

That beautiful, better not go walking slippery docks
alone at night. Stay inside, put up with potheads,
utter pricks. Grin. Bear it when the asshole talks you up.

Virtuous or not, you cannot split off from them,
you cannot individuate, spin night into chrysalis, become –
though, if you could, you'd still be theirs. The path begins

where the wrong turn ends and no way back. It's not only
your car that doesn't start. Trees fall and clutch your legs,
mirrored in the lake, scissoring from birch into a running dive

headlong

through parallel moon

to rock bottom.

Part 3: Die Naked

You will never be forgotten.
Message boards will run

red with your blood, and
aging wolves stalk

your last breath: rent breasts,
belly up in summer mud,

after the rain, outside the tent.
Whoever went off looking

when you thought you heard
a noise remains irrelevant,

pitchforked and heaved
off-screen and into soap operas.

But you will helm conventions,
be sought out for cameos,

lionized on tribute pages,
nipples slapped with dollar signs

to lure the unsubscribed.
By forty, you'll be cast

in filthy habit, Mother
Superior of the ruined convent,

beckoning with baleful eyes
to wayward girls.

Rites

"... I had turned 30, the age for casting out ghosts"
—Susan Swan, *The Biggest Modern Woman of the World*

By 30, of course, I had cast out demons.
Bit of an ordeal – financial health-check, chants,

a spew of bilious nostalgia, proverbial baby tees,
qualms and idiosyncratic oscillations driven out.

In the seventh month, there was a week I sat alone
with hieroglyphed, be-daisied memory boxes

and got over myself sucking face with Asmodei,
riding Geryon into Malebolge, flashing my shit

to summon Ashtaroth, raising the devil's red-
tipped horns to youth gone moderately wild.

Dutifully, I pencilled these things in, recited
the vituperative litanies, erased my tapes,

increased my monthly payments, and disabled
two email addresses at the appointed times.

For years, I lived a nightmare of effusive skeletons,
committing common sacrifice for debts I could not pay.

This kept me stretched so thin I was diaphanous
by day, blending into bricks, banks, public buildings.

But I will not cast out my ghosts. Restless, though benign,
they lend me phosphorescence. Banishment may rouse them

from complacent, seasonal routines. Soft moans barely
levitate the bed. What's a little clot of ectoplasm?

Dorothy

I clang inside myself of late, siren, conflagration,
pitch and twitch as I unstitch my memory,
a golden bolt of trek. My great beaten path:
it nags. The witch I killed. The witches.
Merely vexing parts of me, knocked off

for convenience? Need to slug the wicked ones
who got up in my face? Maybe just road fever.
I could feel her peering through that eye, sick
with grief and envy. How this made her mean.

I felt her sister's death, a sunrise in myself,
proof of my deservingness. I wouldn't be alone,
a friendless stranger. I merited help, my journey
all that mattered. Now I see the truth of it,

that others needed hope, but cannot change
the dream that got me home. Until I came,
they lingered without wisdom, heart, or nerve,
uncertain of their powers. I made sure.

Asteria

goddess of falling stars and night omens

Having been through hell myself,
I sought the hounded and the bold,
hopefuls who would slip the moulds,
forged in lore, to contain them.

Runners who would not be made
to bear a rapist's child, the starving
and the curious. The too kind.
The hopeful, bedevilled with love.

I begrudge no one their passage,
though insist they fall to rise
as otherwordly messengers
through a seeker's night.

Would you become the rock,
mid-sea, to hold a groaning
sister in her pain? Become
the very dirt and say to her

look up when she did scream?
I didn't know I would or could
become a quail and then the earth
to fashion a rough nest to nurse

far greater ones. Might you?
That was years, or hours, ago
if measured by my line, which
doles its lights and firebursts

in its own pulsing time. You
need to make a wish to know
the sanction of my signs. I will
light the sky to ground you,

kiss you wild, set your mind.
In the dark, I whisper guidance.
This is how to fall, I tell them,
so it will make a difference.

Virga

Malum consilium quod mutari non potest.
It's a bad plan that can't be changed.

Relief to see the rain changing its mind,
forced to think again by circumstance,
to lash the distant treeline with its rods

of varied slates on ash, a striking
tinct of want, scrawled in blurry slashes,
building its potential till it cannot

be held back. *Virgule.* Remember
what it means to wait. Especially
at dawn, when all is verge, birdsong

nudging consciousness. Longing,
half-awake, we resist fullness,
knowing it will mean curtailing dream

and warmth let go for good, as once
out into day, our feet will touch ground,
changing us. Sudden storms may

turn us right around, the chilling drop
of some cold revelation send us back
to go within before we leap anew.

II

Eros

From chaos bloomed an inky nub,
a tip, straining out of Nyx's
black-feathered recesses, suckling
on darkness, all wild hair and dart,
cut calf muscles and quads.

Now architect of detailed plots,
the god of love was young then,
slick with placental residue,
drunk on his own effluvium.
Artlessly, he lunged and wheeled,

a glinting, whirling arrow.
Every shard of comet ice he licked
flamed into star, his holographic
palm prints on the surging warp
and weft of chthonic dawn.

Analogies fell from his eyelashes.
His lips, prolific brinks, exhaled
suspension bridges, sung
tensile strands and fluid trusses
across geologic eras,

planted nine day, probing kisses
into stone with quaking lips,
stroked molten, muddy spirals
of crushed rock up into temple,
into gleaming, golden statue.

Libra

The fall arrives with fields of seedy orange womb.
Damn ghost dials up your nerves at 2 a.m.
Pull on a housecoat and answer. *Answer.*

        Slender, wistful tendrils spiral

down around ridged stems, bright greens crunching
in the cold. Helical vines anchor and encircle.
Season of cracked rime and roots exported, votives

        jailed in cavities, monsters ablaze in chasms.
        Our reflective gaze calls down the stars
        and all creation braces, reconsiders.

I can hear the hollow ring of church bells.
Mid-October. *Still?* I think, in morning's chill,
walking through gust after gust.

        Some days I exult in loss,

        stirred up by departing flocks
        as urban doves peck puddle ice,
        rapt by reds and golds.

Ice Storm

It's about what you want, you insisted,
sly in your cocked bowler, playing gumshoe
and I made myself remember: Bastard,
it's about what you want me to want. You.

This goes back to our halcyon days.
We tried to find the time. Gazing
led to orange velour couch, a set piece
I did not know was the standard. Cellared

in a den-like, well-appointed basement
when the elements conspired: ice storm,
power failure, tea lights guttered
then rekindled when our heels touched.

Then the pipes burst. Green-eyed dogs
rushed, bit our naked thighs to warn us
it was raw. People would get hurt – oh
who remembers what was inadvertent

or what clanged too early in the drift-
heaped morning to be recognized as knell?
Gracious after-tasters, we recoiled
judiciously, backpedalled as one.

Missingness

Nine years ago, I titled a poem *Saudade,*
written while I mulled you. It was not
a poem for you, but I did have you
in mind, turning, revolving. At this time

I can't remember what I felt. Even those hungry,
half-cocked lines don't call anything up. I come
back to the word: *saudade.* And it's the word
that conjures – complicates – a gorgeous, I mean splendid

June afternoon. I should just lie down on the grass.
Online, a contingent mocks the moonstruck fuss
over this word. This concept. It comes from the Portuguese.
Maybe the Galician? All we have is "missingness."

Pathetic.

To venture there is all-consuming. I am old enough
to know that this will change and fast. How many dated
selves can you bewail at once? Now another longing
flusters and distracts – the longings: unrelated or

related only for being mine at different times.
Lately they can't seem to coexist, though this has happened –
it's another kind of bliss and burden to be pulled apart
like that, unable to expand. Rough and roiled nights

when lies and mea culpas cluster and confuse. You lie
without meaning to, not knowing how to explain. You try
to explain and the hedge work catches fire in mid-
trim. Mince and cloud. With everything on the line

who would choose to hurt another, all because
of a half-understood, painful sense of wishing you were
somewhere else, a real somewhere, that no longer is,
or never was? The meadow is midtown now.

Syrinx

Pan, caught in a glut
begging play-me
in nightclubs

long ago ditched Syrinx
for the synthesizer's
easy, frequent beat

ditched
in an untrodden place
she trills her lot

as gusts blow
cold and twist
her pliant spine.

Heedless breezes
rustle other reeds,
wend their ways

through a fatigued
and sighing chorus,
who, never immortal,

echo dirges while
they wait in vain
for welcome lips,

deliberate, to move
their battered
bodies into music.

Mechanic Lake

Meghan and I
one summer, we went
topless in a wheat field,
Albert County,
for the cameras (before
smart phones) – burned
the pictures chuckling,

abashed. Well,
we kept a couple
good ones taken later on –
beside Mechanic Lake,
curled across the centre line,
as if asleep, about
to be run over

or discovered,
fallen Pleiades, Meropes
sweating out old grudges
on the scorching road.
I think we both wanted
to scream – our mortal men
fucked off

again. We planned
to hit The Paramount
much later, knew
we'd have to shop
for summer dresses,
watch ourselves, strap
our feet into punishing heels.

Beyond the marsh,
electric towers rose
in their mesh dresses,
holding hands, a paper-
doll chain linked
by wicked voltage.
We were thick as thieves.

Porifera

All sponges do it in the dark:
fullness to fullness, pitted neurotics

bred by sessile generations' sway,
moon-led into marrying their cousins.

The sponge in heat with heft and waft
roils silver clouds, a showboat

flinging seed in underwater smoke,
as spiny mothers collar

what's propelled, to weave a bristled star
into fringed larvae, hard to love,

completely self-absorbed and bound
to the established settlement, by lot,

remaining always open, but walled off
inside themselves, to catch what happens

by and live on that alone. Though
in tough times, mid-dream, some

bloom with gemmules on their own:
podded urchins launched as prayers

or insurance, ragtag cells born to endure.
They wait in the caliginous green depths.

Dorothy II

I am neither murderer nor muse. No one
follows me. I have to count my chickens,
ere they hatch. The dog and I run down
colourless roads. Straw men and contraptions

hear my songs. I sing aloud in fields, kicking
at the posts that mark the borders of our farm
as counterpoint to nothing I can tell them.
I check in on the hens, toss apples to the pigs.

I made that teeming realm and now it ails
inside me, unresolved. Whatever ails in it,
ails in me too. They say that I am wan.
I am the one whose head was hit, and now

I know a world, in trauma born, they don't.
I see that world in them. See the quests
our farmhands could be on, and might be on,
internally. We do not talk of dreams here,

though I know mine to be true. They know
me to have dreamed and laugh me off,
a facecloth to my brow, a kiss, dismissal.
All is well, and they've no time to dither.

Cladorhizidae

Now to soak up Cladorhizidae.
All rancour and nefarious spicule,
they lie in wait for travellers

hauling shells, then lance a spear
into their sides, fix themselves
to pant legs as they pass,

nebulous flypaper. Like paparazzi,
they are spared the indignity
of swallowing their prey, as ushers

pull the soft pulp of their catch
in through the walls, and leave
the hulls to sink, their hosts dissolved

once snared, en route to fresher water,
laboratories, homes in ebbing reefs.
Turn back while you can. Ahead lies

desperation and its measures, stranded
bandits, traps and trappers, wildly
alluring, without a merciful bone.

Material Girl

Been a while since the atom's

forced confession

        bad boy tortured, finally admitting

you were nothing

just one of many

        quarks in the hadron

charming strangers,

bottoms, larks

        how little you mattered

still matter

still want

Nothing's Definite

Fog to encrypt the day.

Self in the rock shimmies,
waves a limpid, patterned arm,

extends a slippery hand,
slinks back into strata.

Mist is the best kisser
anyway, *bonjour.*

How exhausting it is to care,
how cowardly the slew

of disobliging bromides
citing the wrong sources.

Hildegard of Bingen, last I scrolled,
saying let's be sister witches

in the rain. Who are these meme
designers, hitching clickbait

to the dead? I will not share.
None of it is helpful thought,

and spurs an irked, defensive sulk.
I do follow the moon,

waxing now in Taurus,
stubborn, bullish.

Nothing has been carved in stone.
Even stone is nothing.

Mirror in the sky,
I'll fix myself.

Inverted now –
feet in helmets halted

by the gritty, frescoed ceilings
of unrelenting earth.

Scorpio

The chestnuts have been down a month,
gloss gone, cupules decaying. Retired

beauty is ecstatic to be going dark.
Low-grade panic frets about the hedge.

Now the ghostly moon is singing to nuts
and gourds, intoning, chanting, ringing.

This is just the kind of night.
Cold rain beats down on pumpkins,

slicking their rinds. Indentations
form. Dead red berries

cling to balding rowans, stately
in parchment yellow dusk.

They believe in their own return.
Every loss an offering.

The earth will redistribute what
we drop on the gravelled curb.

Somebody will come and pick it up.
Somebody always does.

Finally, we walk with our arms free
to wrap around ourselves,

into the whirling white expanse.
We've been collecting rewards.

Spill

So much of the floor
is drenched by just one
toppled mug, a cup
of coffee soaks

the countertop and seven
feet of tiles, runs under
the microwave, the fridge,

pools to weep
from the counter's lip
into the overfull
junk drawer

III

Terminus

God of limits, please be compassionate.
Fit braces tight to crooked teeth, hold up

the stake that supports our crab saplings,
glove well the fist that pulls up systems.

Thickened skin, slicker, wall of a cell.
A blister. Moat around the open heart

protecting it from doctrines. Keeps on
giving gift of horizon, spheres to eclipse,

gone amok directorates, smouldering,
to surpass. Smash the granite borders.

Let but clouds conceal the crest, whatever
it is I have to get over. Cradle of fear,

nourishing walls of chrysalis. Hair
I will finally climb out of this tower.

Mortal Man

Ships opened the night with blades of flame,
exploding into caves and stars. His father's
smoky, restless hand grazed his as victors shone

in cockpits, cracking wise. Prop and costume
burnt. Every mask a signature, a brand,
a way to judge the men under the capes

and complex jokes. This was seven years before
he broke his nose, fighting off the kind
of dicks who preyed on weaker kids – the frail,

asthmatic sons of single moms – harassed
the grade nine girls with sick come-ons and leers.
Before his father fled: two glasses smashed.

Long before the stabbing, when he stepped,
square-jawed, in between abuser and abused.
Then came the scarred eyebrow, shattered fist,

all charges dropped. A man accused of murder
left the region, taught a lesson, beaten senseless.
It was called the only way – what had to happen,

had to happen. On impact, the sky went fire white
before it blackened. Addled ages, afterwards,
for him to discern greys, to bother looking up

into night's shaded hues for some inhuman, sentient
star's assent, some brave mirror burning bright
inside the starry bruise. I saw him then and wept

to long for life, a body that would die, to trace his hand.
So many who fall this way are left to decompose,
the fitful sky addressed by squads of bloodied mouths,

charity and laughter sheathed beneath fresh scars,
emitting hope enough to breach the darkness and seduce
the waiting doves into descent. I went. Unshackled

from the mournful diadem, I dropped, world by world,
onto the road he follows home, a dawnlit apparition,
luminous and shorn, a trickle of blood from my wing.

At Dusk

What does this full moon portend?
Unlikely pairings, certain sex,

restoration or disclosure,
deus ex or twist?

So. Another coinciding
rise and set. I try not to believe

that's all it is. Another. Don't
forget, dear, I could be blissed

guileless, arched and stark
in dapple. At wit's end.

Inside, our house is loud
with lovers meeting over

corpses, kneeling to inspect
for entry wounds. I can hear them

blaring from the deck, citing
cause of death in synch,

torquing the procedural
to keep each other safe.

I'm sure we'd do no less.
We always wander in

to watch them wipe the knives.
We both know how this one ends.

I rinse my hands conspicuously,
rearrange our spoons.

Early Period in Maine

Halfway to Boston
I slept through Augusta

and dreamt lilacs raced
speedboats opened in clusters

oil watered the flowers
blood sold by the barrel

My uterus filled up
with unrefined diesel

blazing to burn
it would not let me idle

Regrets

Something came up, a pressing emergency. Looks like I might have to go to Alaska. Have you ever been to Alaska? Let me tell you, it is gorgeous in the summer. I have just had a day among days, in terms of awfulness. I finally realized something crushing. So I have to cancel again. And again.

I really did want to come to your thing, you know, get my hair done, everything. Guzzle the bland house red. Cheers, everyone!

My hands are just, as always, too full. My garbage on fire is what's truly happening. Could not have come at a worse fucking time. And the terrible storm of me destined, a downpour, dousing the acrid flames.

I was planning to make an appearance.

In Alaska, in the spring, forget-me-nots swarm the hillsides and roadsides, convivial icons of state. *Myosotis alpestris.* When I was there last, I stared and stared at them, warmed by their cornflower blue. These are the stars of my childhood, actually. I combed Shediac's ditches for patches, and ran home with wilting bouquets, overjoyed to have them. Overjoyed.

They are exactly the same, in Alaska, blooming profusely in cuts of sun, just ten minutes down from the mountains – their stunning, snow-capped ferocity.

So: the open sky grants passage to the light. In the flower lives the sky's indulgence. Is that a very easy relationship? Sky is illusion light scissors like silk, the product of some long-ago, fantastic effort, goading us, often, into our own.

No, I cannot be there tonight. Just not doable. Please give everyone my love. Say hi. Think of me when you drink deep.

Hard Angles

Then again

resistance leads to deeper turpitudes.

On the prowl
for Mnemosyne's kiss,
late at night when the surface

        dips, caves into grotto just for us.

Us. Well.

Finally, all triangles explode
into confounding polyhedrons.

Love coughs its only answer up –
it's an equivocal toad.

In kissing frogs we might –
still might – catalyze a marvel,

though.

Witch of Brookdale

Come to the old subdivision in her gown of gauzes,
a shade in mille feuille and luminous flux,
nacreous berries snagged in her sashes, she favours
a womb in every fold: nasolabial, belly, knee.
A plum in each with a pit in each, instruction in each
but nothing set, how carefully

  she walks, minding deeply, alert to movement
  in every niche. If observed, she would seem to float,
  but never seen, she picks her way through common hedges:
                juniper, myrtle, phlox, holly.

Pause here at the circle of paving stones, backyard char
from a girls' bonfire, torching the ghosts of damned boyfriends:
a sweat sock, a rose and dead baby's breath, condom chucked

to a fit of cackles. Then silence. A simple 'screw him, though.'
Into the ash: a muddy coin, illumination and sanction. On

she walks slowly, dawdling in amber light, dawdling
where the asphalt cracks, arranging it into a puzzle,
glyphed, with one swollen toe, for a nine-year-old

to happen upon, out for the bus in cold half-dark,
beginning to wonder at infrastructure, world-making
in her notes. Pine in her gauzes, birch in her tulles,

lifetimes and lifetimes in bolts of silk, animal chaplets:
bone of goose, bone of duck. A great horned owl
alights on her shoulder,
                flaps, adorns her.

There is a woman out smoking alone.
She senses our rustle and turns.
We can bless her with blind eyes.

Lean against the shed of equipment: rakes and mowers
for mindless tending. A kiss for the wagon that hints
at excursions. Pebble left in it. A scatter of alien seeds
strewn along the length of the trellis.
May whatever survives invite questions.

Into the most ambitious fort:
                    a sliver of meteor, one white feather.

Then, a dimly lit house to visit. Drop a shelled beetle
onto the welcome mat, notice it, open

thrall of children
                    thrall of alarms
thrall of events
                    unfolding unfolding
thrall of the caregiver
                    printed mist
thrall of soil
                    thrall of kitchens
thrall of chronic bodily pain
                    thrall of endurance

                    paint this picture
                    in mirrored shades
                    let shine the aspect

into the house of groans and laughter,
into she who brings it on,

          into he who always delivers
                    into the water of their deep soaker

into the envelope of vinyl
    into the long arcs of poplar
        out of the squared-off yard

limping still from the latest incident,
    pulled to a terribly anxious recipient
        into the easy chair, into the nap

oh cup of tea, oh medication
oh scabbed fist
oh words unsaid and what they could mean
oh swift action about to be taken
here is to finding another way

how she floats in her heavy boots
this torn leaf, *yes* scrawled through maples
divining rod hacked from a branch
rippling ditchwater

drowning grasses
notices traces

        bold as raccoons
        for all to see

Dorothy III

The hens give eggs, not emeralds. I sing
about the sky. I can't sing of myself
or what I know of aftermath, of doubling
back to find the way and have it gone.

Claptrap is the word I heard her use. Oh my.
I could not reimagine my dear aunt.
I needed her at home or there'd have been
no home to strive for. It may be she feels that

and blames me. I blame myself. I let her
have a voice to call my name when I was lost.
And now she will not hear me. Nothing
in that world she could have been but end,

the star I fell from and returned to, head
split open, wanting things to change, wanting
brighter colours, walkways made of brick
from barn to barn, a lion made of stone

to flank the gate, a journey to the fair
at harvest time, sojourns in the city, good
new shoes. For weeks, I made suggestions
and she balked. Suddenly, I wanted curlicues.

I know, I know. Our house had fallen down.
I'd fallen too and with my fall, their fears
rose up like smoke that fills the room
impairing vision. Still, I wish they'd see

the world in colour. Couldn't hurt to paint
the house in blue or red. When it fades,
we'll brighten it again, again, again.
This could be my work, to bring the hues

of hope and bravery to life. My work:
to pull them from my mind into this blight,
this grey we've all agreed to let go on and on,
unchanging, dull and grim. Now I dissent.

To Scale

The organization is tough-minded, firm.
Note the gridwork of steely assistants
testing the rungs of the living ladder.
The gristled floors, the steady clatter.

In the turret, a snake waits to swallow
whoever it is that currently matters,
calloused hand on the splintered lever.
What is required must be willingly rendered.

How can I climb up and over? Once,
I scaled a stony keep, a wary sixteen
in a fit of temper. I knew I had to abscond

from the structure, right away, counting on
the way my knees would buckle under,
when pent-up vigour blew to hinder disaster.

Nemesis

Meeting in the middle
of a bridge on fire:

there is peril.

I will not be a bin
for your notions.

You wield your dead

certainty, a baton.
I have tried and tried

to tell you

I have slogged,
my entire life,

through swamps,

my baton a marsh candle,
a stopgap, only to light

my way. So not a baton.

Sovereign of my islet.
Looming at bog's edge

you lay the lath, insisting
it is my way out,

not your way in. The slat

is kindled by the volley
of our disparate lights.

I want to kick it down.

Of Poison Arrows

A stray nail in the outdoor showers got me.
Four o'clock of a perfect beach day,
I lurched, bleeding, along Dune Lane.
Dad had to hold me down. I lashed

and kicked, pinched his arm, twisted
not to hear the ring of grandmothers
and aunts encircling us, subduing me
with vivid tales of lockjaw, tetanus,

a little septicemia thrown in. I had to let
them pull it from my skin. I was whole
and artless – even happy – singing to myself,
then I was pierced. Wild. Rusting metal

boiled in my heel, a deep dark line
through flesh, blood rushing in to help
and bumping up against it. Had to go,
but I had to be held. Down. Such an

an unpredicted ledge. A gaping sinkhole
in my safe garden. Oh. I am in the plane
crash dream again. Coming, coming,
never comes. I feel it all the same.

No spontaneous abortion or explosion.
Never been. No aneurysm. Never saw
an eighteen-wheeler jackknife on black ice
with no time left to lean into the skid.

I almost did. I almost did. You sat down
with popcorn, spent, on a syringe, jabbed
with blackest magic. Months gone
waiting out the nightmare needle-stick,

the drugs for it that might have done you in.
I wake to fears of that one faulty pin, moronic
gene, the ball I may drop yet. Repeat: most
parachutes open. Stars blink overhead.

Sundew

I'd rather not discuss the tricks I use
to lure them in – the ratio of red lip
to pale cheek, palpability extended
via cocked brow over earthy, organic

bar. I keep a very attractive apartment:
places to fall down and beautiful food,
nothing heavy. I am not obliged to share
what I have gleaned from my study

of light. Investigate for yourself,
if you are so desperate to be let in
on the specifics, honey. I'll tell you
one thing: there's no inside track,

no formula or science, and no meta-
physics. Maybe a little. But no dark art.
Work around nerves, don't trip alarms.
Let them drink deep from your glow.

Tincture

Pull your blessing
up from the deep
earth in a leaf
that will be tea.

Pour the tea
from its clay pot,
cold into your
cupped palms,

raise them
to your waiting
face and look in
the speckled glass.

Heads up. You
are not this
situation. Pull as
hard as you can.

Dorothy IV

Uncle Henry knows more than he says,
I sometimes think. Yesterday, he brought
from town a weathercock, and sat me down
to demonstrate the spin. The wind, he said,

may come from anywhere. We've needed
one of these, it serves a use, and we could stand
to know the wind much better. Pretty though.
I'd say that it will glint atop the house

and catch the sun, surprising us with light,
and it will cast a fascinating shadow, little miss.
But don't go getting lost in darkness, webbed
across the ground, the hay, the grains of feed

that mark our paths. Watch me pound it in
and mind the ladder for me. We've enough
of hit heads on this farm. What I'd dream
if I were hurt would not be so amusing. Careful

now and steady. Easy task enough. I stood
and minded. Nothing fell and it is very lovely.
North and South and East and West are merely
thoughts to me, windlands I will never reach

unless I'm flown. I cannot walk so far, my tattered
shoes not fit. It gets so cold. The roads are dirt.
Rivers cut great lashes through the land. I could
not cross alive, and what would greet me then,

who would take me in or walk beside me, if I did?
I was bound for the schoolroom, but our mortgage
complicates. I might have lingered long among
the books, and ventured there, followed lessons

happily enough, till I could lead a lesson and inject
a heart, a brain, a voice, to speak truth back to charlatans
whirlwinding the words to be their masks, directing us
to wait, continue waiting, war amongst our own

as deadly gales come on, to board up windows,
hide ourselves, as they plunder rainbows,
hoarding gems, reporting nothing of the treasure
back to us. I know the con men well, their mark

upon so many. Few can see because it aches
so quietly and does not shine at all. We think it
part of us. But when I woke to grey, I knew
its lie, legerdemain, a smoky crystal ball.

Effable

Nothing runs between us like translucent nerve
or bloodless silver chord, okay? I wouldn't sense if
you were near me. Take your spiritual connection,
your airs and watery nature, your indeterminacy
and sink into the marsh of the life you deserve.

I know it was a weak goodbye, no great balloon bust,
but helium leaking, a slow bland drift over the province, acre
on acre of trees, waste, and ruts. Finally snagged, all in tatters.
Still I keep you in my feed. I guess that's connectivity,
electricity, complexity, that old something bigger than us

we wanted to have been linked by. Sorry it is effable.
Likely even scrutable, the reason I accept your news,
take it like a horse pill. Dose upon dose to keep in remission.
Just enough to keep the balloon stuck, shreds flapping
in a wind that would return to me anything redeemable.

Half Shell

Oyster tiles were used to hack Hypatia to death,
her genius gutted, snuffed from time and mind.

Thus, we lost an ocean. Hydrometers and astrolabes
shifted under sands, as her life's work

and wisdom – intervals and motions, sundry
clockworks turned to brackish clay

in tidal deeps. *Ostrakon*: a shard of bone,
a tile carved as tax receipt, as writ of banishment.

Imagine waking up to find an oyster shucked,
sucked dry, your goodbye kiss. Since Troy,

we can't deny that love is dangerous and vain,
and there are so few Peregrinas. Ostracize

the lovers, let them die. But ponder this:
Aphrodite rose in glistering froth, daughter

of an old god's warranted castration. Botticelli
stood her in a scallop, obliterating violence.

The truth: a sliver of the shell opened her foot,
and mantic sirens swam through bloody foam,

calling men to sea. That's why I wear heels.
In memory of her little cut, and to make them come

to me and stay, a little longer, in my shell. Pearlescent.
Zinc and salt, her briny, storied wound is mine to dress.

Aren't you just writhing for a deep kiss, even still?
Come on. I will feed you strawberries, it's safer.

Sagittarius

We met in that blizzard and fucked with abandon.
Ha. It was the season of synthetic reds and purple dyes.
You had to shovel us out. I just wanted to believe

for half a minute. No such luck. Nothing left to give away,
I didn't think you'd call. You called but it meant nothing.
It was just too close to Christmas. Wasn't funny. I know

I was open, far too . . . feeling it all through me. Didn't you?
This year, just a flurry: did you know that stripping down
and dancing with our derelict might be the act of a saint?

I want to see you, need to see you. Look: even trees have stripped
in the wind, last leaves shaking like rags from knobby, obscene,
protruding bits, and slap-slapping our faces. We can be bold,

pom-puffed revellers in the sleet, and how very sad of us
it would be to stay in, when there are bawdy, Rabelaisian tales
to give the gift of, Santa hats and microbrew, plushy laps,

war stories and work put off, the sudden, merry, drunken beauty
of us falling down and rising up like we could still be one. Hum.
Violet nights of crystal snow have finally come to persuade us.

Egyptian Cotton

I am forty, in Linens, remembering you.
A vapid, headlong Shangri-La lub-
dubs its way from heart to palm,

nape to knee, as souvenirs cartwheel
loose in the gut – that wrecked us?
Obdurate second brain. A thought:

every day, old seashells turn up
in the mountains. This proves something.
But what? We were young

and in bed, moving in tandem, even
as we pushed and kicked apart. Butterfly
inked on curvy hip, kiss on cheek

that would never be washed. This store
is cool and looks so clean. Beautiful
amenities – throws embroidered

with peacock feathers, irises and eyes.
Eiffel Towers. Street names. Buttercups
in all my synapses, hot, gold blaze

of the sun, returning. A summer
to relive. Soap dishes of reckoning.
That it was glorious, that it was.

I want things so much, I could slash
my fingertip, rush to the watershed
under the twelfth red moon.

Dinner

If you love me you will not say
spongiform or *prion* at the dinner table,

will not bring up these grisly murderers
bent on contortion and driving us crazy.

Forget how careful we are at the borders.
You will not acknowledge such pitiless undoing.

If you love me, you will know, tonight,
I can only discuss destiny, miracles against all odds,

beautifully transgressive marriages and the spirit world

breaking through
                        proof

Capricorn

I will want to have it both ways,
every time. Takes a good man
to intuit how the both ways dovetail
into quiet afternoon, bills paid up
and babies rocked before news
of a storm provokes a storm
and starts me hurling strategies
into the fought-for calm.

You will have to have a real job
and some savings, cash in hand,
the bloody palms of come from nothing,
ladder slivers in your toes, the awkward
manners of the often overlooked,
song on your lips, a hint of dew,
but have it in you to intimidate

coyotes (say it *kiiiii-oats*),
when they show up, sorry-assed,
on our stoop. You must learn
to understand them too. I am only
one part maenad, but house a slew
of troubled worlds and want to live,
intently, among all that I have learned
to keep at bay for my own good.

Malabsorption

The human sponge
is not born an invertebrate.

Flagella wild and plentiful
enough to handle webs

spun thick for harvest, heart-
warming enough to guarantee

a bandwagon, a fandom.
Something in us feels through,

sees through signage, can
manage long campaigns

until a baneful meme gets stuck.
A calculated poison, lodged,

inflames what was intrinsic
and integrity is lost. A woman,

who'd been still, begins to wring
her hands inside your heart,

her image and story warped.
It never quite clears up.

Rhythmic lies and half-truths
clog the microtubules,

old mascara clumps
in captive organelles

calumny slithers through.
And you can't stop believing.

Shortcut

Men under trucks and a small Tim Hortons:
possibly mirage. Everything on wheels is up

on cinder blocks or pucks. The road from nowhere
so gone with potholes, flocks of bathing titmice startle

up at our approach, every half kilometre, doves out of a hat.
We are being swallowed by a serious grey green, the green

on grey of rock and tree, of moss on bark, of road signs,
faint and falling down, sinking, and the bloody red

of spray-canned dates and teenage braggadocio paled
to driveway gravel pinkish. Driving like we've only got one wheel,

off-kilter, favouring the right. Bumps and shocks have leached
our little fortitude. The road is in our teeth, its scattershot,

its pebbles held beneath our tongues. The knuckles don't go
literally white. We barely speak. I watch the gauge like a hawk.

Hallway

Cold, dark September morning, before
we have turned the heat back on,
I limp groggily, one leg still asleep,
in a dopey beeline, down the unlit hallway

to the kitchen, where I can tell you
have coffee on. You come lumbering
from the shower, towel at the waist,
rubbing your neck, and we collide,

my head into your bicep. Graze
you from your nipple to
your navel with two nails,

pointless on warm, damp skin,
and we stand in the perfumed fog
ten seconds, maybe longer, swaying
a little bit, your body holding me up.

Echo

You watched me like an eagle with that knife,
certain I would press too hard

and ruin the dining room table:
do you have it in you to be gentle?

I was worried sick about my own increasing
roughness, a recklessness of spirit I could not

subdue. I hid from it with you, hurt and still
unsure of how to craft a cautious promiscuity,

too wise and yet not wise at goddamn all.
I was never certain what you knew.

We watched murdered woman mysteries
and smoked, drank only tea, crafted and worked

puzzles late into the nights. You let me be.
Now could you send the spine I need to hide

my fears, as you hid yours, from those I hold
most dear, that they may grow to face themselves

in safety I provide, just being here? Hello?
I hand down your recipes and tricks, supply

the glue, repeating *this is how you make it, press*
down here, but not too hard, your echo still.

Crook

Hammocks of light
strung from sun to ices –
warped from the go.

The string bows into
three-day moon, bent into long-
ing for the past

as it recedes from view.
One particle of rose
subverts the love.

We're less symmetrical –
a bulging chrysalis,
backs to one another.

Charlottetown, July

I sleep in a sand gritty bed,
kicked by my oldest boy.

The ditches of PEI are blooming
under a purple sky – beach peas
and wild roses banked, lupins

going skeletal. Feel them on the wind.
Hot as hell, we plod to the beach.

Would that I could stretch my legs.
Would that I could relax. Trouble is –

You won't be happy, sings Gilbert to Anne,
if you wear the wrong flower to the dance.

Anne required, longed for, a lily. A flower
she could live with. Buttercups nod,

a crane alights. Vetch all over clambering.
A raccoon digs through our cache of shells,

out under maples, right downtown.
A siren, a call – *Would you hang on, man?*

My little love hangs onto me. I move, move,
just a little. Tiger lilies agape in hollows.

Over the bridge: my life's ideal.
Willows, books, the moon bright and full
over graveyards and refinished gables.

After Flooding

Having, all day, drunk the deluge, hurried,
half-said news of it, I find my eye
for resemblances is tired, gritty with debris –
city wrack exacerbating what is almost sure
to become chronic dry eye or blepharitis –
Did you know, did you know, the sign insists
on asking, this is a disease? Incurable disease.
Smug pronunciation. Now you know.

Here is a drop, though. Drops and drops.
Helps a little with what can't be helped.
It has been forever since I cried. All but
forgotten the irritation, evidence of pain.
So this wicked wind comes on over the mess
of bricks and mortar. Leaves, twigs
pulp from the river, shredded on pave.

I am angry you've disappeared. Hurt,
sad, whatever, whatever. This is like
nothing, resembles nothing – well
I do see faint echoes in the trash-strewn,
sodden grass. Still it will go green, soon
this sudden pool will seep into the ground
we will gather on to celebrate another

reality, subculture, deep culture, history,
milestone, lie – the arts. Not you and I, but we
in general. We, with family, with friends,
all the community I can claim, all I can
offer my children: this world and the shape
of things. You will be elsewhere, whether
or not this long silence breaks, whether or not
it matters how high, in the end, we rose.

Astraea

In the distance,
she unbound the ladders
of gold from her star,
unwilling to return –

the fields that flourished
with good works gone
all to iron, to arms
to horrible striving.

How to wash away
the blood of murdered
mothers, shepherds,
horses, cradled

those last days
of unreason,
gardens gone
to graveyard

no realm for her
to bless, no justice
to be had amid
such stupidness.

It was mad and cruel,
that world of men
amassing tonnage,
let the poets sorrow

as they might,
let women fight,
let children dream
until brought

to the slaughter.
Now only the slap
of violent storms
might reconfigure

hope as muscular
as greed, might force
together, bring
together fighters

sickened by the fight
amid her emblems:
maiden, caduceus,
corn broom, vial,

shards of her intent
ranged out of order
on tossed coasts, shell
and stone scrubbed

blue and bone white,
glimpses of perfection
in the asters sprigging
wild from the headlands.

Samaras

It is time for winged things to wheel.
Brittle, feathered keys emerge in crooked pairs

bound by a ropy kiss. Head to head, minds met,
dancing partners set to tumble in euphoric lockstep

with the late spring winds, as sparse red maple
branches tap the windows, tempting dwellers

with the long fine fingers of a vine imp tasselled
with translucent leaves, their waxy velvet

nothing like the bitten bark, thickset limbs
and nests they are determined to conceal.

Down spin the copters, dizzily. Whirling too,
we split them open, clumsily, tearing them

apart, stick them on our noses, hang them
from our lobes. Twirl and they are lost. Well.

They were star-crossed, wind-crossed, meant
to go their ways. We're mechanism only,

not at fault, also building lives, surging up
and out to be propelled, we hope, on such a love,

just once before we fall in artless heaps, to be
taken up at leisure, if at all, before the long, cold

lonely tunnel down into the serious abyss
of earth and ice we've only just begun to sense.

Dorothy V

The crops come up, enough for us, girdled
in bright greens. There is green in my eyes,
though mixed with greys. And still more colours
there. And yellow in the sky, most days,

where sun pierces the clouds, beaming down
to earth through amber dust that dances midst
the rows we tend. I stomp, it circles up
and up, a mirror storm, my cyclone, making

light of what light's done to earth. The grit
gets in my hair, it stings my eyes, it weathers
my two dresses, wears our skin. There has
to be a veil, I've come to think, imperfect,

leaking variegation through its pores, lending
tones and gleams to what's familiar, recreating
what we know too well. Something of its sight's
lodged in me now. I can't see like before,

all's doubled, all means twice, or even more.
I live to help my aunt, to help and serve
as comfort. She knows what she knows,
and there is sorrow there. Without me, it would

gather in her bones. I'm possibility. I'll pull
it from myself to make a path from greyness,
wish by stone, too bright to be lost on. Safe,
as real as home. I'll start with this pliant coil.

Acknowledgements

Thanks to the editors who included poems from this collection in their publications – *The Antigonish Review, Poetry is Dead, The Hamilton Arts and Letters Review,* and *The Puritan.*

Serious thanks to Kerry-Lee Powell, whose badass encouragement helped propel me to complete this manuscript. Thanks also to Shoshanna Wingate for the support and magical conversation. Thanks also to this collection's editor, Garry Thomas Morse, for the careful attention to each line.

Most especially, thanks to my friends – in particular Brad, Nicolle, Meg, and Liz – who propped me up with numerous long conversations as I worked on this collection. Your voices, insights, and kindness are in here.

JENNIFER HOULE grew up in Shediac, New Brunswick – though she was born in Massachusetts, just north of Boston. Her poems have appeared in numerous literary journals and her work has won several awards. Her first book, *The Back Channels,* which won The Writers' Federation of New Brunswick's Alfred G. Bailey Prize for best poetry manuscript, was published by Signature Editions in Spring 2016. It went on to win the J.M. Abraham East Coast Literary Award for best Atlantic Canadian collection of poetry and was shortlisted for the League of Canadian Poets Gerald Lampert Memorial Award for best first collection. A lifelong Maritimer, Jennifer now lives just outside of Fredericton with her husband and two sons. Committed to promoting literacy and bilingualism among youth, she sits on the board of Word Feast: Fredericton's Literary Festival, and is an active member of her local writing community. She was named one of 18 Canadian women writers to watch by CBC Books in 2018.

ECO-AUDIT
Printing this book using Rolland Enviro100 Book instead of virgin fibres paper saved the following resources:

Trees	Solid Waste	Water	Air Emissions
2	78kg	6,394L	258kg